# KAY FAIRFAX

# Stir–fries

*Photography by Simon Wheeler*

WEIDENFELD & NICOLSON

# Kay Fairfax

Kay Fairfax is widely known in the world of food and flowers of the southern hemisphere. Her home town for many years was Sydney, Australia, where she ran a catering business, wrote for magazines, made a range of children's toys and appeared on television.

In Bowral, New South Wales, she owned and ran a florist shop and counted many celebrities amongst her clientele. She has written books on food, decorative crafts and horticulture, including *Homemade*, *The Australian Christmas Book* and *100 Great Stir-fries*. She now lives in Wiltshire.

# Contents

The urge to entertain,

to open our doors to our friends

and to give them

the best fare we can provide

is deep and good.

DESMOND BRIGGS

# Introduction

Stir-frying was until recently equated with Oriental cooking. Now, as our cultural and culinary horizons have widened, and ingredients from every corner of the globe have become available, stir-frying has no limits. It is quick, easy, inexpensive and nutritious. Any type of food can be cooked by this method: meat, poultry, fish, seafood, rice, noodles, vegetables and fruit. Only a small amount of oil is used and because of the high heat and rapid cooking time the flavours and nutrients are sealed in, and the food retains its texture and crispness.

Most cooks have come to realize that the wok or stir-fry pan is an essential piece of equipment in the kitchen: it is the right cooking medium for today.

The recipes I have chosen for this book are very versatile and are designed to demonstrate the range of food that is suitable for stir-frying. Now you can create a taste sensation in less than one hour from arriving home to sitting down to an inspired meal.

# WARM SEAFOOD SALAD

**SERVES 4**

200 g/7 oz squid tubes (fresh or
   frozen)
200 g/7 oz uncooked prawns
200 g/7 oz scallops (fresh or
   frozen)
2 tablespoons fish sauce
2 tablespoons groundnut oil
1 Cos or Iceberg lettuce,
   shredded
2 garlic cloves, crushed
a handful of fresh basil,
   roughly torn
salt and pepper
1 small red chilli, deseeded and
   thinly sliced

Split open the squid tubes, remove the backbone and clean thoroughly. Lay flat and trim the wide end of any tough pieces. Pat dry with paper towels. On the upper side of each piece, make a small crisscross pattern, about 1 x 1 cm/½ x ½ inch, not cutting right through the flesh. Cut into pieces about 5 x 5 cm/2 x 2 inches. Shell and devein the prawns. Clean the scallops. Put the fish sauce in a small jug with 2 tablespoons water and mix well.

Heat a wok or large pan, then add the oil. When the oil is hot and begins to smoke, add the lettuce and stir-fry for 2 minutes. Remove with a slotted spoon and place on a serving dish in a warm place.

Add the garlic to the wok and stir for 30 seconds. Add the squid and stir-fry for 2 minutes; the pieces will fan out and begin to curl up into small tubes. Add the scallops and prawns and stir-fry for 2 minutes. Add the basil and a little salt and stir for a further 1 minute. Add the sauce mixture and stir for 1 minute, then finally stir in the chilli and some freshly ground black pepper. Serve immediately.

*The seafood served on its bed of lettuce needs no accompaniment. Follow it with fresh figs and cheese, or a red plum or peach sorbet.*

# VEGETARIAN STIR-FRY

**SERVES 4**

2 tablespoons groundnut oil

2 garlic cloves, crushed

2 teaspoons grated fresh ginger

125 g/4 oz fresh asparagus tips

125 g/4 oz green beans, sliced,
  or small broad beans

125 g/4 oz mangetout, tips
  removed

125 g/4 oz courgettes, thinly
  sliced diagonally

1 red or orange pepper,
  deseeded and cut into strips

125 g/4 oz button mushrooms,
  sliced

3 spring onions, finely sliced

12 pitted black olives, cut in
  halves

1 tablespoon light soy sauce

1 tablespoon chopped fresh basil

1 tablespoon chopped fresh
  parsley

50 g/2 oz pine nuts, toasted

salt and pepper

2 teaspoons sesame or basil oil

Heat a wok or large pan, then add the oil. When the oil is hot and begins to smoke, add the garlic and ginger and stir for 30 seconds. Add the asparagus and beans and stir-fry for 2 minutes. Add the mangetout and courgettes and stir-fry for 1 minute. Add the pepper and mushrooms and stir-fry for a further 2 minutes, or until the vegetables are tender but still crisp.

Add the spring onions and olives and stir-fry for 1 minute. Stir in the soy sauce, herbs and half the pine nuts. Season to taste with salt and pepper, add the sesame or basil oil and stir for 30 seconds. Sprinkle with the remaining pine nuts and serve immediately.

*This is a meal in itself, but is also great as an accompaniment to roast chicken or grilled chicken breast. Follow with an apple or rhubarb crumble.*

# PRAWNS, PESTO AND CORIANDER

**SERVES 4**

12 large uncooked prawns
3 tablespoons olive oil
4 tablespoons pesto
a small bunch of fresh coriander,
    finely chopped
salt and pepper

Shell and devein the prawns, leaving the tails on.

Heat a wok or large pan, then add the oil. When the oil is hot and begins to smoke, add the prawns, pesto and coriander and stir-fry for 30 seconds. Lower the heat and stir-fry for 2−3 minutes. Season to taste with salt and pepper. Serve immediately.

*This makes a fabulous starter or a lunch dish served with rice or a green salad. Follow it with a fresh fruit salad, or cheese, grapes and strawberries.*

# Spinach, bacon and mushrooms

**SERVES 4**

450 g/1 lb spinach or Swiss
   chard
1 tablespoon groundnut oil
2 garlic cloves, sliced
2 rashers of lean bacon,
   chopped into strips
125 g/4 oz button mushrooms,
   sliced
2 tablespoons pine nuts,
   toasted

Wash the spinach and drain well. Chop into large pieces.

Heat a wok or large pan, then add the oil. When the oil
is hot and begins to smoke, add the garlic and stir for
30 seconds. Add the bacon and stir-fry for 2 minutes,
or until the bacon is nearly crisp. Add the mushrooms
and stir-fry for 1 minute. Add the spinach and stir-fry
for 3 minutes, or until the spinach has wilted. Add
the pine nuts and stir-fry for a further 2 minutes.
Serve immediately.

*Serve as a vegetable side dish, along with new potatoes, to
accompany grilled steak, pork or veal escalopes. Follow with a
compote of peaches and plums.*

# MONKFISH IN BLACK BEAN SAUCE

**SERVES 4**

450 g/1 lb monkfish, cod or
  hake fillets, cut into bite-sized
  pieces
4 tablespoons black bean sauce
4 tablespoons fish stock
2 tablespoons light soy sauce
5 thin slices fresh ginger
1 small red chilli, deseeded and
  thinly sliced
1 tablespoon groundnut oil
½ red or orange pepper,
  deseeded and cut into strips
125 g/4 oz mangetout, tips
  removed, then sliced in half
  diagonally
salt and pepper

Prepare the fish, removing all the bones. Place in a bowl with the black bean sauce and leave to marinate for 10 minutes. Put the stock, soy sauce, ginger and chilli in a small jug and mix well.

Heat a wok or large pan, then add the oil. When the oil is hot and begins to smoke, add the pepper and mangetout and stir-fry for 2 minutes. Add the sauce mixture and stir for 2–3 minutes. Using a slotted spoon, remove the pepper and mangetout and keep warm.

Lower the heat and add the fish pieces; stir carefully for 2–3 minutes, depending on the size of the fish. Season to taste with salt and pepper and serve immediately, with the vegetables. Pour any remaining sauce over the fish.

*Vegetables are included in this recipe, so all that is needed is a base of rice or noodles. Have an indulgence to finish – chocolate mud cake or crème brûlée, or for the more health-conscious a selection of cheeses and fresh fruit.*

# GARLIC CHICKEN LIVERS AND BACON

**SERVES 4**

450 g/1 lb chicken livers,
    cleaned and chopped
1 tablespoon pale dry sherry
2 teaspoons cornflour
1 tablespoon groundnut oil
1 garlic clove, crushed
1 onion, finely diced
3 rashers of lean bacon, finely
    diced
2 teaspoons chopped fresh
    chives
2 teaspoons chopped fresh
    parsley
pepper

Put the chicken livers in a bowl and pour on boiling water to cover. Drain and repeat this process two or three times. This will eliminate any bitterness. Drain well and pat dry with paper towels. In a small jug, combine the sherry, cornflour and 2 teaspoons water.

Heat a wok or large pan, then add the oil. When the oil is hot and begins to smoke, add the garlic and stir for 30 seconds. Add the onion and bacon and stir-fry for 1 minute. Add the livers and stir-fry for a further minute.

Remove the wok from the heat and add the cornflour mixture. Return to the heat and stir for 1 minute. Add the chives and parsley and stir for 30 seconds. Serve immediately, with freshly ground black pepper to taste.

*An indulgent breakfast for special occasions, a terrific dinner party starter or light lunch. For lunch, serve with a mixed leaf and herb salad, followed by fresh melon or tarte tatin.*

# CHICKEN, MANGO AND AVOCADO

**SERVES 4**

450 g/1 lb chicken breast, cut
   into strips
4 tablespoons mild mango
   chutney
1 tablespoon groundnut oil
2 fresh firm ripe mangoes,
   chopped into bite-sized pieces
2 firm ripe avocados, chopped
   into bite-sized pieces
salt and pepper.

Put the chicken in a large bowl with the mango chutney and leave to marinate for 10 minutes, turning several times to ensure the chicken is well coated.

Heat a wok or large pan, then add the oil. When the oil is hot and begins to smoke, add the chicken and its marinade, and stir-fry for 3–4 minutes. Remove any large pieces of chutney with a slotted spoon. Add the mango pieces and stir-fry for 1 minute, then add the avocado and stir carefully for 2 minutes, or until the mango and avocado are hot through but still firm. Season to taste with salt and pepper. Serve immediately.

*An easy dish to make the most of when mangoes and avocados are in season. Serve on a bed of steamed white rice with a green salad. Serve a sweet dessert such as crème caramel or chocolate or orange mousse.*

# QUAIL AND WATER CHESTNUTS
## *in oyster sauce*

**SERVES 4**

4 quail

salt and pepper

2 tablespoons oyster sauce

1 tablespoon light soy sauce

1 tablespoon pale dry sherry

2 teaspoons cornflour

1 tablespoon groundnut oil

1 large garlic clove, crushed

½ red pepper, cut into thin strips

½ green pepper, cut into thin
strips

50 g/2 oz mangetout, trimmed
and cut into thin strips

125 g/4 oz button mushrooms,
thinly sliced

125 g/4 oz tinned water
chestnuts, rinsed and sliced

Clean the quail and pat dry. Chop each quail into 4–6
pieces; a meat cleaver is ideal for this. Rinse well and
dry with paper towels. Place in a bowl and season with
salt and pepper. In a small jug, combine the oyster and
soy sauces, sherry, cornflour and 1 tablespoon water.

Heat a wok or large pan, then add the oil. When the oil
is hot and begins to smoke, add the garlic and stir for
30 seconds. Add the quail pieces and stir-fry for 4–5
minutes, until well browned. Remove the quail with a
slotted spoon and keep warm. It may be necessary to fry
the quail in two batches; if so you may need to add a
little more oil to the wok.

Reheat the wok and add the peppers, mangetout,
mushrooms and water chestnuts. Stir-fry for 2–3
minutes. Remove from the heat, add the cornflour
mixture and stir for 2 minutes. Return the quail to
the wok and stir-fry for a further 3 minutes, or until
the meat is hot. Serve immediately.

*This is a wonderful dinner party dish and as it includes
vegetables it can be served with no other accompaniments than
rice or sliced boiled potatoes sprinkled with a little chopped
fresh parsley or dill. It is not too rich and spicy and could be
followed by strawberries in Kirsch – or Brie and figs.*

# HONEY DUCK AND CRACKLING

**SERVES 4**

450 g/1 lb duck breast
1 teaspoon Chinese five-spice
   seasoning
2 tablespoons honey
2 tablespoons light soy sauce
2 tablespoons Worcestershire
   sauce
1 tablespoon pale dry sherry
1 teaspoon cornflour
1 tablespoon groundnut oil
1 garlic clove, crushed
1 teaspoon grated fresh ginger
2 spring onions, thinly sliced
   diagonally
2 tablespoons sesame seeds,
   roasted
1 teaspoon sesame seed oil

Remove the skin from the duck and cut it into 5 mm/ ¼ inch strips. Cut the meat into 1 cm/½ inch thick slices and season with the five-spice seasoning. In a small jug, combine the honey, soy and Worcestershire sauces, sherry and cornflour.

Heat a wok or large pan, then add the oil. When the oil is hot and begins to smoke, add the duck skin and stir-fry for 2–3 minutes, until crisp and golden. Remove with a slotted spoon and drain on paper towels.

Reheat the wok and add more oil if necessary. Add the garlic and ginger and stir for 30 seconds. Add the duck meat and stir-fry for 3 minutes. Remove the wok from the heat and add the cornflour mixture, return to the heat and stir for 2 minutes. Add the spring onions and stir-fry for 1 minute. Add half the sesame seeds and stir for 30 seconds. Add the sesame seed oil and stir for 1 minute. Remove from the heat, sprinkle with the remaining sesame seeds and serve immediately.

*This dish is quite rich and would be best served with fresh green beans and steamed rice or sliced boiled potatoes. Follow with a fresh fruit sorbet or homemade citrus fruit ice-cream and almond bread.*

# PORK WITH MUSHROOMS AND OLIVES

**SERVES 4**

450 g/1 lb pork loin fillet, cut
   into 5 mm/¼ inch thick slices
pepper
2 tablespoons oyster sauce
1 tablespoon soy sauce
1 tablespoon dry white vermouth
2 tablespoons cornflour
1 tablespoon groundnut oil
125 g/4 oz broccoli, cut into
   small florets
125 g/4 oz button mushrooms,
   sliced
½ orange pepper, cut into thin
   strips
12 black pitted olives, sliced into
   thirds

Prepare the meat and season with pepper. In a small jug, combine the oyster and soy sauces, vermouth, cornflour and 2 tablespoons water.

Heat a wok or large pan, then add the oil. When the oil is hot and begins to smoke, add the meat and stir-fry for 2 minutes, or until the meat is brown. (The pork may need to be cooked in batches, in which case more oil may need to be added.) Remove with a slotted spoon and keep warm.

Add the broccoli to the wok and stir-fry for 2 minutes. Add the mushrooms and pepper and stir-fry for 2 minutes. Remove the wok from the heat and add the cornflour mixture. Return to the heat and and stir for 1 minute. Add the olives and return the meat to the wok and stir-fry for 1–2 minutes, until the meat is hot. Serve immediatley.

*A colourful dish that needs only white or brown rice to make a complete meal. It is not rich so you could follow it with a fresh apple or pear tart.*

# ROSEMARY AND GARLIC LAMB
## *with rice*

**SERVES 4**

125 g/4 oz long-grain white rice
1 tablespoon groundnut oil
2 large garlic cloves, sliced
450 g/1 lb lean lamb fillet, cut
    into 5 cm/2 inch strips
3 large sprigs of rosemary
2 teaspoons Pernod
salt and pepper
3–4 spring onions, sliced
    diagonally into 5mm/¼ inch
    lengths
1 teaspoon rosemary oil

Cook the rice until it is tender. Drain well, spread on a plate, cover and refrigerate to allow the grains to cool and separate. This will prevent the rice from becoming sticky.

Heat a wok or large pan, then add the oil. When the oil is hot and begins to smoke, add the garlic and stir for 30 seconds. Add the lamb and rosemary and stir-fry for 3–4 minutes, until the lamb is browned. Add the Pernod and 2 teaspoons water and stir for 1 minute. Remove the rosemary. Season to taste with salt and pepper. Add the cold rice and stir-fry for 2 minutes. Add the spring onions and stir-fry for 1 minute. Add the rosemary oil and stir for a further 30 seconds, then serve immediately.

*This is a strongly flavoured dish that includes rice, so all it needs to set it off is a fresh green salad, or perhaps bunches of thin green beans tied together with a chive. Follow with a refreshing lemon mousse, or oranges in Cointreau.*

# Beef with citrus sauce

**SERVES 4**

2 tablespoons freshly squeezed
    orange juice
grated rind of ½ orange
1 tablespoon pale dry sherry or
    dry vermouth
2 tablespoons dark soy sauce
1 teaspoon cornflour
1 teaspoon Chinese five-spice
    seasoning
2 teaspoons soft brown sugar
1 tablespoon groundnut oil
1 garlic clove, crushed
1 teaspoon grated fresh ginger
450 g/1 lb fillet steak, cut into
    1 cm/½ inch thick rounds
150 g/5 oz asparagus tips
150 g/5 oz chestnut
    mushrooms, sliced
salt and pepper

In a small jug, combine the orange juice and rind, sherry, soy sauce, cornflour, five-spice seasoning and sugar. Mix well to dissolve the sugar.

Heat a wok or large pan, then add the oil. When the oil is hot and begins to smoke, add the garlic and ginger and stir for 30 seconds. Add the beef and stir-fry for 3 minutes, or until the meat is browned. (The beef may need to be cooked in batches, in which case more oil may need to be added.) Remove with a slotted spoon and keep warm.

Add the asparagus and mushrooms and stir-fry for 2–3 minutes. Remove the wok from the heat, add the beef and the cornflour mixture and stir well. Return to the heat and stir-fry for a further 3 minutes, until the vegetables are cooked but still crisp. Season to taste with salt and pepper. Serve immediately.

*This has a lovely fresh flavour and needs only plain rice as an accompaniment. As it is light and not too rich, you could serve almost any dessert afterwards; summer pudding or pears poached in red wine would echo the freshness of the flavours.*

# The Basics

## TECHNIQUES AND TIPS

Stir-frying is one of the oldest methods of Oriental cooking, but it is very well suited to today's health-conscious cooks because it uses very little oil and high heat, so the ingredients cook quickly and retain as much as possible of their vitamins.

Once started, the process should not be stopped, so all ingredients must be prepared before starting to cook (see next page). All the meat and vegetables should be chopped into pieces of uniform size, and all liquids should be mixed together in a jug, so you can pour them into the pan with one hand while continuing to stir with the other.

Always heat the wok or pan first, before adding the oil. When the oil is very hot and begins to smoke, add the first ingredients.

Ingredients such as vegetables may be varied according to what is available; if you are making substitutions, follow the weight suggested in the particular recipe.

When adding a cornflour sauce mixture it is a good idea to remove the pan from the heat for a few seconds to help ensure that there are no lumps in the sauce.

If the mixture looks dry, add a little water, stock, sherry, vermouth or citrus juice. Do not add more oil as the food will absorb it and burn.

Have hot plates ready in the oven and serve as soon as possible, as vegetables rapidly lose their crispness.

# EQUIPMENT

It is best to buy a wok at least 30–35 cm/12–14 inches in diameter as it is easier to toss food around in a large pan. Before buying a wok, check that it is suitable for your heat source. Traditional Chinese round-bottomed woks work on gas hobs but not on flat electric ones.

A high-sided deep frying pan may be used instead of a wok, but make sure it has a long, flameproof handle. The cooking time will vary according to the type of pan you are using. Successful stir-frying requires accurate preparation, using sharp knives or a cleaver.

The correct spatulas, shaped for your wok or pan, and a long-handled slotted spoon make the cooking much easier and more enjoyable.

# INGREDIENTS

**MEAT**

Always cut meat across the grain. Meat to be stir-fried needs to be as dry as possible, as it must fry and not steam. For this reason fresh meat should be used and not frozen meat, which tends to become watery when it is thawed.

Buy the best quality, lean meat available. Stir-fry recipes use relatively small proportions of meat to vegetables, so this is not an extravagance and makes all the difference to the end result. Many meats can be substituted for each other: beef for pork, chicken for duck or turkey.

**FISH**

Buy the freshest available and use uncooked prawns when possible. Most seafood is interchangeable in these recipes, or use a combination instead of just one variety.

**VEGETABLES**

Use the freshest vegetables you can, and look for seasonal bargains. Vegetables can readily be substituted for each other: try Chinese greens such as bok choy in place of spinach or Swiss chard. When using lettuce choose a crisp variety such as Cos, Iceberg, or Little Gem. Remember to add vegetables in order of cooking time required.

Slice vegetables diagonally as this allows more of the surface to come into contact with the heat, and therefore cooks them faster. Broccoli should be broken into small florets and the stem peeled and cut diagonally into thin slices.

Always wash your hands well after handling chillies, or use rubber gloves and do not touch your face, especially your eyes, as this can sting. The longer chillies are cooked the more flavour and heat they produce, but the longer garlic is cooked the more flavour is lost.

## HERBS

In many stir-fry recipes, fresh herbs (rather than dried) are essential.

## RICE

Rice to be stir-fried should be precooked and cooled; it can be kept in the refrigerator for up to 4 days. This ensures that the grains are dry and remain separate. Serve soy sauce separately as it tends to discolour the rice if added during cooking.

## OILS, SAUCES AND SPICES

Groundnut or peanut oil is best for stir-frying as it can be heated to a high temperature without burning and has a neutral flavour. Do not add sesame or flavoured oils until the last minute as they tend to burn and are used for flavour only.

Spices should be as fresh as possible and only unsalted nuts should be used.

Bottled sauces such as hoisin are an invaluable addition to some stir-fried recipes. Taste before using as their flavours are distinctive and often strong and salty. Chilli sauces vary greatly in their 'heat', so be careful not to add too much.

## MENU PLANNING

It is difficult to begin the meal with a starter when you are serving a stir-fry for the main dish, unless you are being informal and sitting around the kitchen table. Otherwise there will be a long pause between courses while you disappear to stir-fry, and unless there are two of you at the stove it is virtually impossible to serve more than one stir-fry dish at a time. Instead, I suggest you concentrate on presenting really good fruit and cheese or a dessert that you have prepared in advance.

# Classic Cooking

### STARTERS
**Jean Christophe Novelli** Chef/patron of Maison Novelli, which opened in London to great acclaim in 1996. He previously worked at the Four Seasons restaurant, London.

### VEGETABLE SOUPS
**Elisabeth Luard** Cookery writer for the *Sunday Telegraph Magazine* and author of *European Peasant Food* and *European Festival Food*, which won a Glenfiddich Award.

### GOURMET SALADS
**Sonia Stevenson** The first woman chef in the UK to be awarded a Michelin star, at the Horn of Plenty in Devon. Author of *The Magic of Saucery* and *Fresh Ways with Fish*.

### FISH AND SHELLFISH
**Gordon Ramsay** Chef/proprietor of one of London's most popular restaurants, Aubergine, recently awarded its second Michelin star. He is the author of *A Passion for Flavour*.

### CHICKEN, DUCK AND GAME
**Nick Nairn** Chef/patron of Braeval restaurant near Aberfoyle in Scotland, whose BBC-TV series *Wild Harvest* was last summer's most successful cookery series, accompanied by a book.

### LIVERS, SWEETBREADS AND KIDNEYS
**Simon Hopkinson** Former chef/patron at London's Bibendum restaurant, columnist and author of *Roast Chicken and Other Stories* and the forthcoming *The Prawn Cocktail Years*.

### VEGETARIAN
**Rosamond Richardson** Author of several vegetarian titles, including *The Great Green Gourmet* and *Food from Green Places*. She has also appeared on television.

### PASTA
**Joy Davies** One of the creators of *BBC Good Food Magazine*, she has been food editor of *She, Woman* and *Options* and written for the *Guardian, Daily Telegraph* and *Harpers & Queen*.

### CHEESE DISHES
**Rose Elliot** The UK's most successful vegetarian cookery writer and author of many books, including *Not Just a Load of Old Lentils* and *The Classic Vegetarian Cookbook*.

### POTATO DISHES
**Patrick McDonald** Author of the forthcoming *Simply Good Food* and Harvey Nichols' food consultant.

### BISTRO COOKING
**Anne Willan** Founder and director of La Varenne Cookery School in Burgundy and West Virginia. Author of many books and a specialist in French cuisine.

### ITALIAN COOKING
**Anna Del Conte** is the author of *The Classic Food of Northern Italy* (chosen as the 1996 Guild of Food Writers Book of the Year) and *The Gastronomy of Italy*. She has appeared on BBC-TV's *Masterchef*.

## Vietnamese Cooking

**Nicole Routhier** One of the United States' most popular cookery writers, her books include *Cooking Under Wraps*, *Nicole Routhier's Fruit Cookbook* and the award-winning *The Foods of Vietnam*.

## Malaysian Cooking

**Jill Dupleix** One of Australia's best known cookery writers, with columns in the *Sydney Morning Herald* and *Elle*. Author of *New Food*, *Allegro al dente* and the Master Chefs *Pacific*.

## Peking Cuisine

**Helen Chen** Learned to cook traditional Peking dishes from her mother, Joyce Chen, the grande dame of Chinese cooking in the United States. The author of *Chinese Home Cooking*.

## Stir Fries

**Kay Fairfax** Author of several books, including *100 Great Stir-fries*, *Homemade* and *The Australian Christmas Book*.

## Noodles

**Terry Durack** Australia's most widely read restaurant critic and co-editor of the *Sydney Morning Herald Good Food Guide*. He is the author of *YUM!*, a book of stories and recipes.

## North Indian Curries

**Pat Chapman** Started the Curry Club in 1982. Appears regularly on television and radio and is the author of eighteen books, the latest being *The Thai Restaurant Cookbook*.

## Barbecues and Grills

**Brian Turner** Chef/patron of Turner's in Knightsbridge and one of Britain's most popular food broadcasters; he appears frequently on *Ready Steady Cook*, *Food and Drink* and many other television programmes.

## Summer and Winter Casseroles

**Anton Edelmann** Maître Chef des Cuisines at the Savoy Hotel, London, and author of six books. He appears regularly on BBC-TV's *Masterchef*.

## Traditional Puddings

**Tessa Bramley** Chef/patron of the acclaimed Old Vicarage restaurant in Ridgeway, Derbyshire. Author of *The Instinctive Cook*, and a regular presenter on a new Channel 4 daytime series *Here's One I Made Earlier*.

## Decorated Cakes

**Jane Asher** Author of several cookery books and a novel. She has also appeared in her own television series, *Jane Asher's Christmas* (1995).

## Favourite Cakes

**Mary Berry** One of Britain's leading cookery writers, her numerous books include *Mary Berry's Ultimate Cake Book*. She has made many television and radio appearances and is a regular contributor to cookery magazines.

Text © Kay Fairfax 1997

Kay Fairfax has asserted her right to be identified
as the author of this Work.

Photographs © Simon Wheeler 1997

First published in 1997 by
George Weidenfeld & Nicolson
The Orion Publishing Group
Orion House
5 Upper St Martin's Lane
London WC2H 9EA

British Library Cataloguing-in-Publication data
A catalogue record for this book is available from the
British Library

ISBN 0 297 82277 2

Designed by Lucy Holmes
Edited by Maggie Ramsay
Food styling by Joy Davies
Typeset by Tiger Typeset